BIRD MAZES

Patricia Wynne

Dover Publications, Inc.
New York

*The author wishes to thank Ilil Arbel,
who helped out considerably in
the creation of this book.*

Bibliographical Note

Bird Mazes is a new work, first published by Dover Publications, Inc., in 1994.

International Standard Book Number: 0-486-28112-4

Manufactured in the United States of America
Dover Publications, Inc., 31 East 2nd Street, Mineola, N.Y. 11501

Note

As you work the mazes in this book, you will become acquainted with 46 birds of the wild. These fun (and challenging) mazes ingeniously combine realistic, informative drawings and crafty puzzles. For instance, you will help a great blue heron find his way through a watery path to his favorite dinner: a fish in shallow water. In this way you will learn the environs, diets and curious habits of the ostrich, the kiwi, the kingfisher and the waxwing to name but a few. You will also find yourself smack-dab in the middle of some of the cleverest mazes you've ever tried. The solutions begin on page 50 in case you get lost, so let's get started! Your feathered friends await!

The great blue heron is going fishing in shallow water. Start at the heron and find a clear path to the fish.

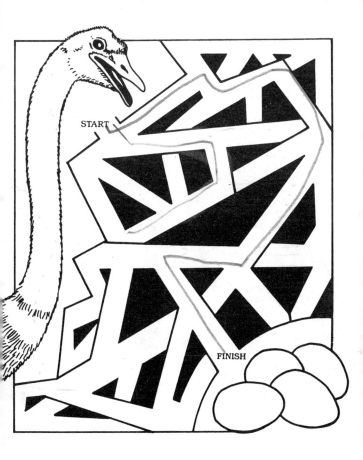

START

FINISH

Father ostrich wants to incubate his giant eggs. Lead him to them.

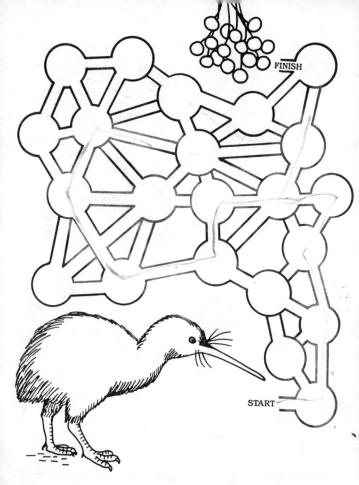

Help the kiwi smell his way to the delicious berries.

The swimming green-winged teal must fly through the clouds and join his migrating friends.

7

The chimney swift has to reach the chimney where it will build a nest.

FINISH

START

Help the honey badger find the greater honey guide at the beehive.

9

START

FINISH

The white stork, returning from a winter in Africa, must reach its rooftop nest in Europe.

10

START

FINISH

The cardinal just noticed some nice sunflower seeds on the ground. How can he get to them?

11

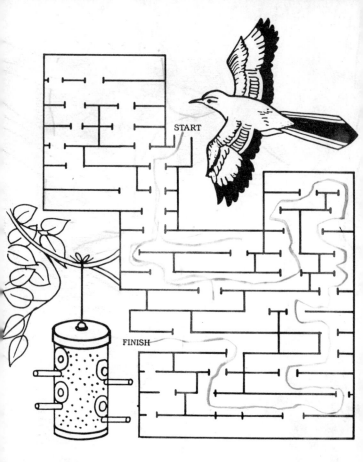

START

FINISH

The mockingbird is flying from her home at the forest's edge to visit your backyard feeder. Help her!

START

FINISH

The nuthatch climbing down the tree trunk must catch the insect on the branch.

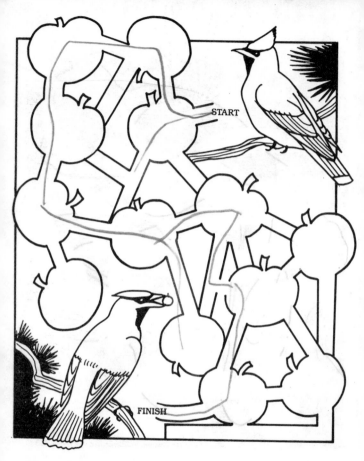

START

FINISH

The cedar waxwing at the top wants to join his friend for dinner. Follow the right path through the berries!

START

FINISH

The kingfisher wants to go to her eggs in the underground burrow. Lead her there.

15

Someone built a special house for the bluebird. Help her get there to start her nest.

16

When the goldfinch finishes bathing he will preen on the tree branch above him. Get him there.

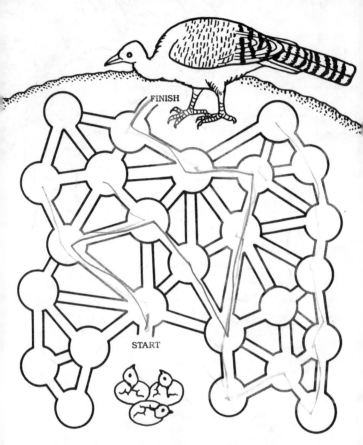

FINISH

START

The mallee fowl's chicks are hatching in their earth-mound nest. Help them join their mother at the top of the mound.

18

The Arctic tern can fly so fast that, although she is now visiting the penguins in Antarctica, she will get to the puffin in the Arctic in the same year—if you lend a hand!

The cockatoo likes the nut he is eating. Help him reach all the other nuts on the lowest branches.

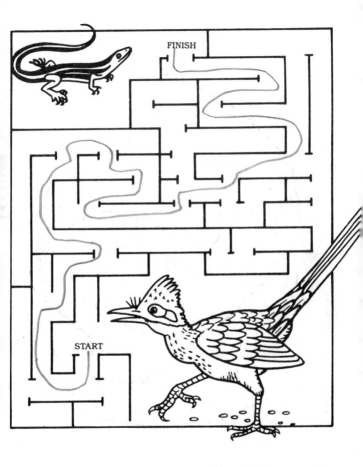

FINISH

START

How fast will the roadrunner go through the maze to catch the lizard?

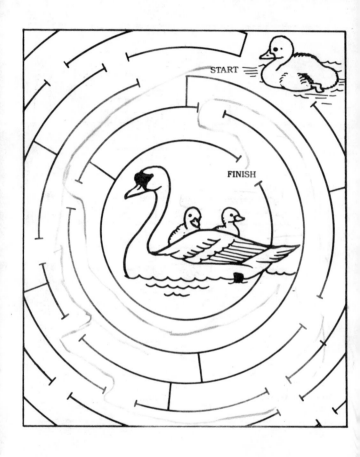

The cygnet is trying to find his mother, brother and sister mute swans. Can you help him?

START

FINISH

The hummingbird must reach the beautiful flower to drink its nectar.

START

FINISH

Can you help the laughing gull reach the water surface, where he can find his dinner?

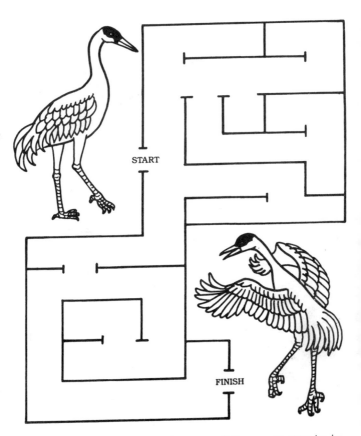

START

FINISH

The sandhill crane at the top of the page wants to come down to dance with his friend. Which way will he come?

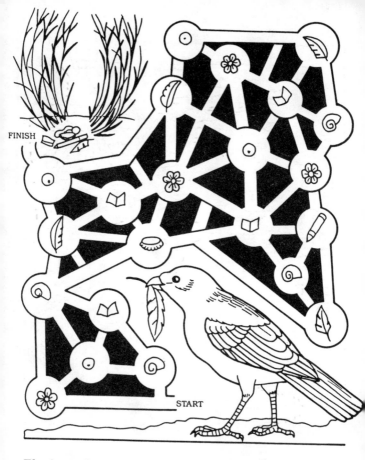

FINISH

START

The bowerbird needs to reach his bower, on the way collecting objects to decorate it.

START

FINISH

Help the black-capped chickadee get to the cattail plant—one of his favorite winter foods.

27

The golden eagle parent needs to catch the rabbit for dinner.

28

The flying pigeon must wing her way through the clouds to her friend on the window ledge.

FINISH

START

The snowy owl nests on the snowy, cold ground. Her mate, who has caught a mouse, will bring it to her with your help.

The male wild turkey is puffing out his chest and fanning his tail to impress the hen who must come through the maze to join him.

31

The black-headed weaver from Africa is collecting grass. Help him bring it and add it to his nest.

START

FINISH

How fast will the swooping pelican catch the fish in the ocean?

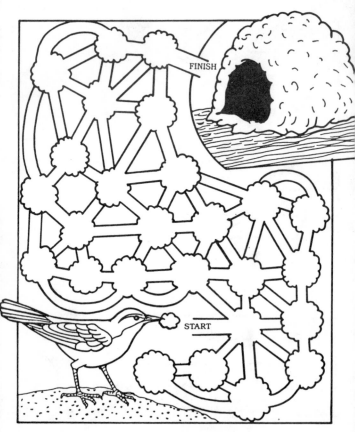

Help the rufous ovenbird from South America reach her nest, while collecting clay balls from which to build it.

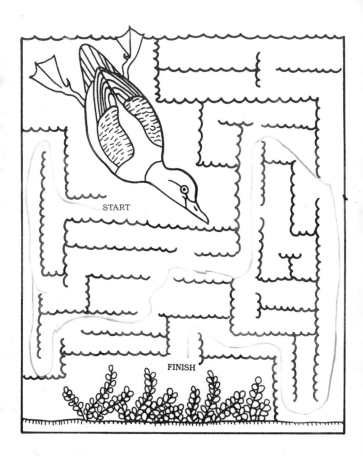

START

FINISH

The pochard feeds on plants at the lake bottom. Can you help him get there?

START

FINISH

Help the incoming crow find her way to her friend on the ground.

START

FINISH

The cuckoo is trying to reach a reed warbler's nest.
She wants to lay her own egg in it!

37

FINISH

START

It's a long way from the Arctic tundra to the pinecones in your neighborhood, but with some help from you the snow bunting may pay a visit this winter!

The tailorbird has made a nest from leaves and fibers.
Now that she has gathered sticks to put inside, help
her get back.

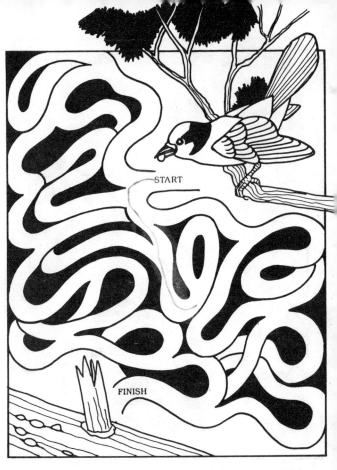

START

FINISH

The gray jay sticks seeds into the bark of special trees. Could you help him reach the tree at the bottom?

40

FINISH

START

Help the penguin at the bottom leap out of the water and join his friends on the shore.

FINISH

START

The downy woodpecker must climb to the top limb of the tree.

START

FINISH

The European song thrush needs help to catch the snail and break its shell on the rock.

43

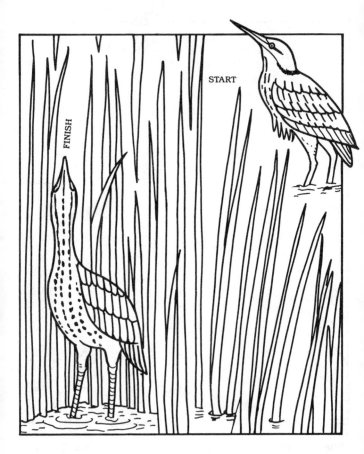

Can the bittern at the right find her friend hidden in the pond reeds?

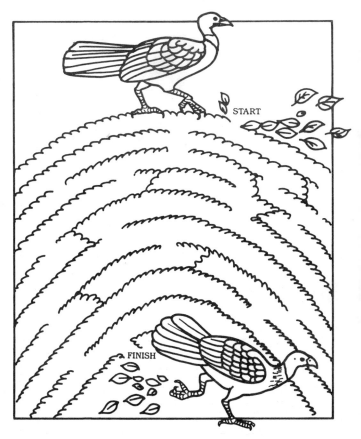

The Australian brush turkey and its mate are building a mound of leaves as a nest for their eggs. Help the one on top meet the one below to finish the mound.

45

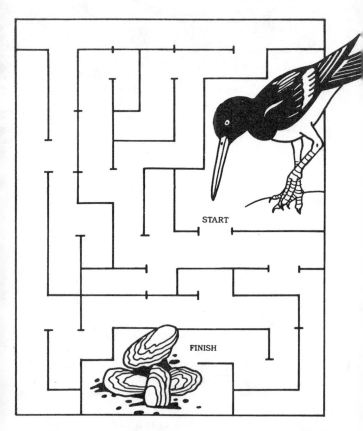

START

FINISH

An American oystercatcher uses his long red bill to pry open oyster shells. Lead him to them.

46

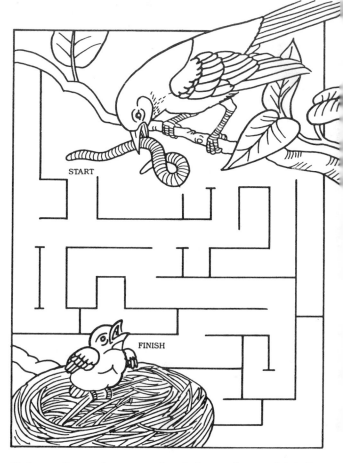

START

FINISH

Help mother robin go to her baby and serve him the delicious worm for breakfast.

Which one of the things at the top is the long-eared owl hunting in the middle of the night? Lead him to what he wants.

The puffin at the top would like to join his friend for lunch. Can you show him the way?

Solutions

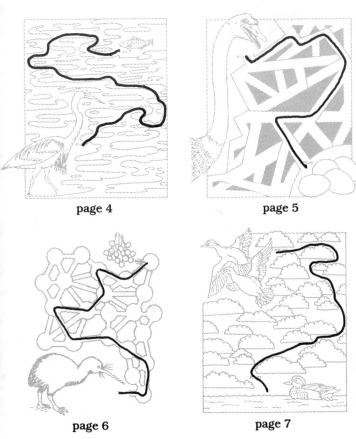

page 4

page 5

page 6

page 7

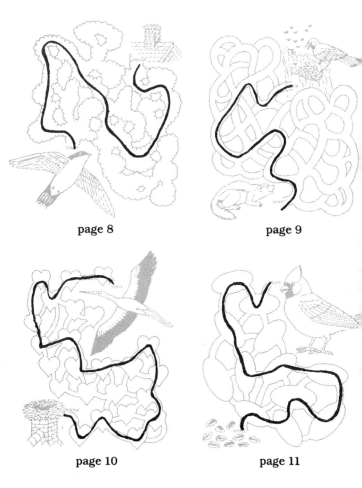

page 8

page 9

page 10

page 11

51

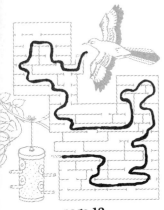

page 12

page 13

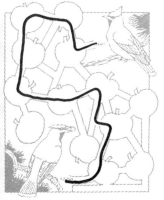

page 14

page 15

52

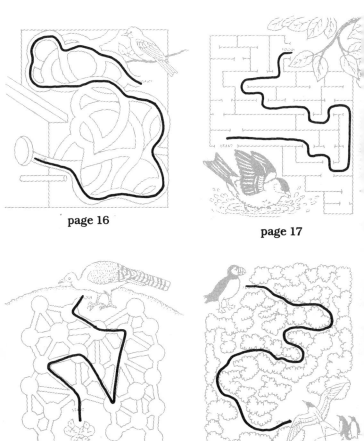

page 16

page 17

page 18

page 19

page 20

page 21

page 22

page 23

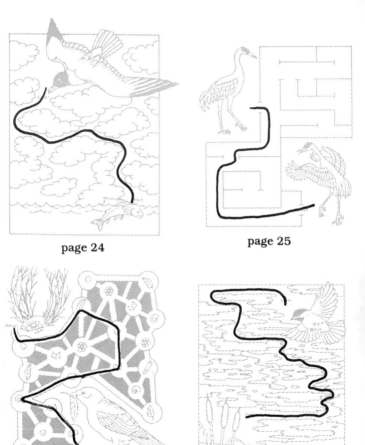

page 24

page 25

page 26

page 27

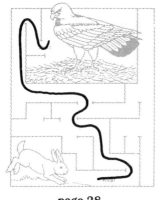

page 28

page 29

page 30

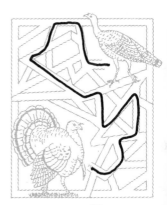

page 31

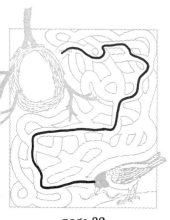

page 32

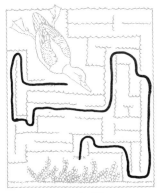

page 33

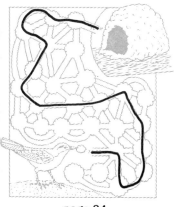

page 34

page 35

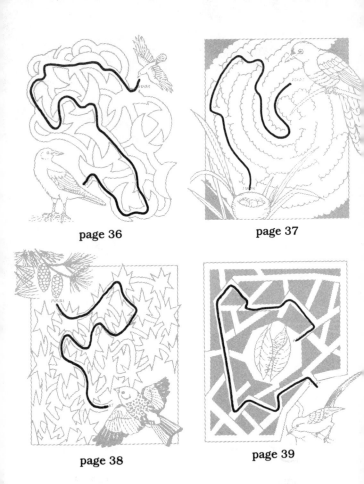

page 36

page 37

page 38

page 39

page 40

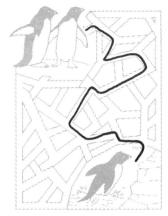

page 41

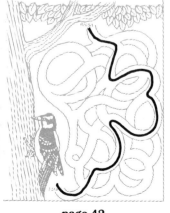

page 42

page 43

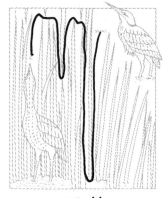

page 44

page 45

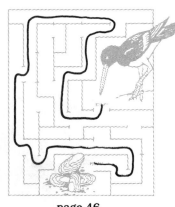

page 46

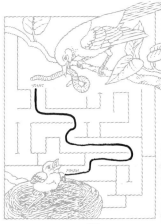

page 47

60

page 48

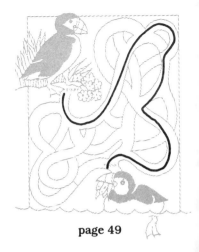

page 49